FADING SHADOWS

FADING SHADOWS

Library of Congress catalogue card number 73-620142

Pruett Press, Boulder, Colorado

PREFACE

The early 1800's witnessed a diversified group of trappers, hunters, and military personnel that penetrated the plains and mountains of an early Territory from which the State of Colorado was established on August 1, 1876. Dominated by roaming Ute, Arapahoe, Sioux, Commanche, and Cheyenne Indians, this was a land of yet to be discovered potential wealth and multiple challenges. By 1843, wagons slowly and dangerously traversed the rugged country toward the Pacific Coast. Such crossings were further stimulated subsequently by the California gold strikes in 1849. Ten years later (1859) placer gold deposits and rich lodes of gold, silver, copper, lead, and zinc were rediscovered in the mountainous regions of pre-Colorado, where wild and turbulent days prevailed until the early 1900's. Englishmen, Swedes, Danes, Norwegians, Mexicans, Indians, Chinese, Italians, Irishmen, Frenchmen, Poles, Russians, Hungarians, and Germans came to dream, dig, and die for elusive minerals.

Towns and camps of every size, composition, objective, and design suddenly appeared. Ocherous mine and prospect dumps, mills, aerial tramways, trails, and roads appeared on hillsides and in valleys. Clear streams became contaminated and silt laden. Then in 1872, came the railroads to link the more prominent towns and camps.

Saloons, fancy parlors and vivacious women, assay and survey offices, supply depots, law and newspaper offices, boarding and opera houses jockeyed for position on main and back streets. Lynching, claim jumping, epidemics, Indian raids, murders, shootings, robberies, blackmail, fires, bankruptcies, speculations, and promotional intrigues evented the time. Smallpox, diptheria, and bronchial infections expanded cemeteries. Fortunes were won and lost; many men and families became disenchanted only to try again in other remote and virgin areas.

By the early 20th century, most of these early boisterous and colorful mining camps had faded into oblivion—a few remain today and have attained matronly dignity. Those that failed to prosper and continue their activity are reflected now only by decaying scattered log cabins, tumbling foundations, broken wagons, tilted headframes, collapsed tram towers, unattended cemeteries among the aspen, rusting ore cars and tracks, and deep-rutted roads and trails.

FADING SHADOWS is only a partial photographic story of some of the relics of this colorful, square-nail mining era, many of which, will be lost during the next 50 years (or less) to vandalism, snow, ice, wind, avalanches, fires, floods, mill ponds, salvage, highways, and termites. For historic details of early Colorado towns and camps the reader should consult references given on the following page.

Photographs in this book were selected from 1000 pictures taken by the authors during the past 4 years. People within each are living ghosts— men who once were cold and wet underground, those that hauled heavy timber and machinery over narrow mountain passes, built towns and camps, and kept mills in operation—women who knew the complexity of unattended childbirth, sickness, mine accidents, and isolation. We hope the reader hears and feels the presence of these silent people of which only a few are alive today.

L. W. LeRoy
J. J. Finney

Golden, Colorado
1973

ACKNOWLEDGMENTS

To D. A. Linn LeRoy, special acknowledgment is given for the line sketches throughout the book, for a number of photographs, for contributing to the book format, and designing the jacket and cover.

To Professor George W. Johnson, Colorado School of Mines, the senior author is indebted for his comments and interests in editing the verse sections of the book.

The authors are grateful for the references listed below which served as indispensable guidance based on years of field and office historic research.

Perry Eberhardt, 1959, 1968, *"Guide to the Colorado Ghost Towns, and Mining Camps"*—Sage Books, Denver, Colorado.

Robert L. Brown, 1963, 1968, *"Jeep Trails to Colorado Ghost Towns"* —Caxton Printers, Ltd., Idaho.

——————————, 1969, *"Ghost Towns of the Colorado Rockies,"* Caxton Printers, Ltd., Idaho.

——————————, 1972, *"Colorado Ghost Towns—Past and Present,"* —Caxton Printers, Ltd., Idaho.

Muriel S. Wolle, 1949, *"Stampede to Timberline,"* Published by the author, Denver, Colorado.

To the Colorado School of Mines Foundation, Inc., the authors are indebted for the financial support of FADING SHADOWS in conjunction with the Colorado School of Mines Centennial, 1974.

RECOMMENDED READING

Those wishing to obtain better understanding of mineral deposits, the books listed below are recommended.

S. M. Del Rio, 1960, *"Mineral Resources of Colorado,"* Colorado State Mineral Resources Board, Denver, 763 p.

E. B. Eckel, 1961, *"Minerals of Colorado—A Hundred Year Record,"* U. S. Geol. Survey Bull. 1114, 399 p.

C. F. Park, Jr. and R. A. MacDiarmid, 1964, *"Ore Deposits,"* W. A. Freeman and Company, California, 475 p.

It is suggested that those planning to seriously visit and better appreciate Colorado's mountainous areas, secure topographic quadrangle maps (U.S. Geological Survey) from the Map Section, Federal Center, Denver, Colorado.

DEDICATION

To the nameless thousands that contributed to the discovery and development of the mineral wealth of the Rocky Mountains.

CHANGE

Hundreds of early mining camps
  And towns of the middle and
Late 1800's of the area now
  Western Colorado were birthed
By rich deposits of gold, silver,
  Lead, zinc, and copper.
Today, beryl, clay, coal, feldspar,
  Molybdenum, uranium, mica, iron,
Fluorspar, perlite, pumice, tungsten,
  Oil, gas, and rare earths
Add to the State's economy.
  Mining ventures, small and large,
Through the years have fluctuated;
  Many have collapsed because of
Supply and demand, depletion, variations in
  Deposit values, and production costs.
The time has come when high-grade
  Ore concentrations are a rarity.
Prospecting has entered a phase
  Demanding a well-organized, systematic,
And costly approach to new discoveries.
  The days of "hit-and-miss" search
Methods of a 100 years ago are
  Part of the past.
Modern prospecting requires
  Careful analyses and mapping of
Rock types, rock relationships, and
  Rock structures and more
Concern is being directed to complex
  Chemical and physical conditions
Under which deposits formed.
  In these early days, geologists,
Mining engineers, geochemists,
  Geophysicists, drilling and blasting
Technicians, and metallurgists were
  In the background or yet to appear.
Only "yellow ground", crude assays, and colors
  In a pan incited early
Prospectors to mark corners
  Of claims, make filings, and
Build cabins, to be questioned
  A hundred years later by those
Who marvel at their determination,
  Frustration, and hope to find the
Deeply hidden ores that,
  Too, are rapidly fading.

Cabins, walls, mills, and tunnels of the 1800's are among the FADING SHADOWS of this book

1

THE MOUNTAINS

We were born 70 million years
    Ago — raised from the depths
To heights above the clouds.
    Glaciers, rivers, and winds have
Carved our cliffs and divides, and
    Rock and mud have filled our valleys.
Volcanoes have covered us with
    Soft gray ash, and molten
Magmas have flowed upon us.
    Our colored bands are bent and
Broken, and the forces
    Still change our slopes and ridges.
Hot waters have brought to us
    From below, minerals
For which men seek and mine.
    In the Fall, leaves turn to
Yellow, gold, brown, and red —
    'Tis then our humble best is offered.

Roberts—1971

2

In the winter, heavy snows blanket the rocks of Lincoln Peak in the Mosquito Range

On a rocky slope this lonely sentinel for decades has resisted severe storms

Yankee Boy Basin, ice-filled 50,000 years ago, lies above timberline in the San Juan Mountains

Yule Pass lies notched in the skyline and through which the road leads to Marble

Across a glacial basin, a winding road climbs to the Whale Mine in Hall Valley

7

THE MOUNTAIN AND THE CABIN

A million years
Or more
Ice flowed and scraped
Its flanks, and glaciers
Filled its deep ravines.
Plunging streams etched
Its ridges and broken
Rocks tumbled
Down the valley.
Its crown is high
And reaches for the
Morning glow that wakens
The silence, covering
Lonely cabins
Of a hundred years.
It is I, the mountain, that
Can tell a longer story — listen.

Roberts—1972

Silent cabins are dwarfed against Mount Democrat — a fourteen thousander

Bleached cabin among boulders from a crumbling cliff

From an 1860 cabin a view toward the Continental Divide

Bunkhouse near Mineral Point in the San Juan Mountains

Mill office reflects a sunset and merges with shadowed mountains

It witnessed hundreds of years at timberline before the miners came —
this gnarled Bristle-Cone Pine in late afternoon

THE BRISTLE-CONE PINE

For decades pitch-filled cones
    Have grown on branches
Reaching for the sky and
    Under where the Ute
Made camp and awaited
    Buffalo, deer, and elk
In the nearby marshy meadow.

Then came bearded
Trappers to pause in its shade,
    Then cattle, sheep, and horses
To graze on slopes below.
    Passed it miner's trekked
In search of hidden fortunes.

Roberts—1972

MOUNTAIN PEAKS

Below us — ragged timberline
Above us — infinity and space
Around us — tapering shadows
Within us — quiet and
Secrets of a million decades.

Roberts—1972

Among cabin timbers, a loner stands against snow-patched peaks

On its way to collapse

Doomed to collapse in coming years, stands this once proud place of business in Ashcroft

Filled with ore rock that will never see the smelter.

Not many standing today after 70 years

Square nails parade along a ridge pole

Locked for a hundred years this barn of hand-hewn logs

After decades they still hold

Rusting barrow on the slopes of Red Mountain

No longer do sour-dough bread and biscuits come from the oven

They rolled over Gunsight Pass in the high country

Its turning days belong to the past

*The old town of Eureka in the San Juans still has **character***

AN OLD TOWN

There's little left of me
    On the valley floor —
Only broken cabins,
    Rutted streets and paths,
Empty windows, doorless doors,
    Rusting iron, and purple bottles.
A hundred years ago
    Dim lanterns cast a

Glow upon the grass,
    Mart and Sue picked flowers,
Men climbed to mines,
    Whiskey flowed,
Wagons creaked along trails, and
    The hawk searched the night.
Let an old town rest and
    Claim these thoughts.

Roberts—1972

Through the window came many thoughts of someone

A FORGOTTEN NAME

He remembered silence in the forest
    Reaching into the turquoise sky,
And flowers along the stream
    Tumbling from the melting snows.
He remembered rolling clouds
    Across the mountain ridges
And unspoken words on winds
    Rolling down the valley.
He remembered morning frost

    Sparkling in a rising sun
And echoes of laughter
    Jumping up the rocky slope.
Now his home is but a wall
    Clinging to a barren cliff
Where time projects its call
    From broken window sills
And frameless empty doors
    Into space of fading shadows.

Roberts—1972

An empty window in Nevadaville

Warped door of a prospector's cabin in a land of wind and cold, above timberline

Beginning of the end of Sts. Johns

Where winter snows are 20 feet and avalanches roll and tumble

An engineer designed sturdy timber supports for the Sunnyside Mill

Early morning shadows and a nail silhouette

An owner's pride in the wild town of Silvercliff of 1880

On a blizzard-swept plain

Silent hinges at 13,920 feet

Bulging to a maximum — an ore bin

Wall and window of the 1860's at Nevadaville

Fire destroyed many mines, camps, and mills in the early days

THE FIRE

The drill steel stuck,
    The air went dead, and
The wet heat was 108.
    Four lamps flickered
In darkness against
    The broken face.
Smoke rolled from the shaft,
    "Let's get da Hell outa here,

Dis Son-o-Buck ain't the
    Mornun fog.
Up dat ladder, Nat, and take
    Da left cross-cut,
Den down da drift
    To tunnel leben."
All Deacons, now, these four.

Roberts—1970

Toothed wheels lifted gold ore and men from deep shafts

Doorless furnace fronts stand among debris of a burned mill at the Tomboy Mine

Handmade belt wheel turned spiral cams to raise heavy ore-crushing stamps

39

Wooden belt wheel no longer turns the shaft

Once a store and hotel at Midway

Under London Mountain, rich deposits of gold and silver

Only the floor remains of a prospector's cabin on the crest of the Mosquito Range.

In an Engelmann Spruce forest at Sacramento

Only the stairs of a bunkhouse remain after a snow avalanche

One of the best in Animas Forks, the gateway to Cinnamon Pass in the San Juan Mountains

45

Far above timberline in the Mosquitos

Bleached boards reflect a morning sun at 13,960 feet on Horseshoe Peak

Pine and aspen share the sunrise with this cabin front

After winter, spring is near at Turret

Bay-windowed house at Sneffels

A stately relic at Crystal hides among the trees

Feed stall in a square-nail barn is no longer protected from heavy winter snow

THE MILL

On steel-thread cables,
    Buckets of ore glided
To the mill in the
    Valley below.
Rock crushers broke silence;
    Wheels and shafts turned;
Heavy timbers shook;
    Ridged tables vibrated, and
Iron in troughs
    Claimed green copper.
From cyanide fluids came
    Yellow gold, and
Gray mud silted the stream.
    The mill with
Empty windows, fallen roof, and
    Broken beams, clings
To the valley slope.

Roberts—1971

Cables hold part of a mill collapsed by winds and snows near timberline

San Juan Chief Mill at timberline near Engineer Pass, San Juan Mountains

Revenue Mill on a mountain slope stubbornly resists time

Buildings transported from early towns are now tourist novelties in Fairplay

After 60 years in the San Juans

Terraced foundations of a mill and golden aspen at Gladstone

Snowslides may someday claim the operating Pandora Mill in the San Juans

Against a stormy sky, ore buckets suspend in space

Valueless rock cones below the mill at Red Mountain

Shrine-like tram tower pierces a cloudy sky at the Yankee Girl Mine

Aerial tram tower on the slope of Mount Bross, is draped with rusting cables

Cables in tension support a Pennsylvania Mine aerial tram tower on a talus slope

Headframe looks westward across the Wet Mountain Valley to angular peaks of the Sangre de Cristos

Headframe at Nevadaville against a moonlit sky

Wheels turned and cable wound to surface ore from a deep shaft at the Portland #1 Mine

Proud but deserted Yankee Girl Mine in the high country of the San Juan Mountains

The cable no longer lifts the ore bucket

Horse-drawn grinding mill (Arastra) used by Spanish miners in the early 1800's

Arastra base in the stream bed of Buckskin Creek

THE BUNKHOUSE

The wind rolled, the snow fell, and
    Coffee steamed on the stove.
From the fireplace, shadows played
    Across bunks and boots.
Then with fury
    The snowslide came
From the mountain above
    To claim the house and all
Within its weathered walls.

Roberts—1972

After a snowslide but little remains of the bunkhouse

71

Two terrace levels of a hillside mill destroyed by snow avalanches

Ladder to the sky at the Monte Cristo Mill near Breckenridge

Superstructure gone, a gold-dredge platform floats in its pond

No longer its dredge buckets carry gold-bearing gravels to the table separators

Power pole reverently watches across slopes and valleys of the San Juan Mountains

THE DANCER

The blood of Chica Cortez
    Came from many lands —
Some from the jungle
    Of Nicaragua,
Some from the plateau
    Of Old Mexico,
Some from the bay
    On a swampy coast,
Some from the street
    Of a nameless town, and
Some from the hills
    In far-off Spain.
Blood boiled
    As she danced and laughed
On the pine-board floor
    Of a dim-lit hall
In Buckskin Gulch,
    A century ago.

Roberts—1971

Dance hall where Chica Cortez could have entertained in 1862

Deployed infantry of square nails rise from a weathered dance floor

THE MOUNTAIN AND THE MINER

They blasted my sides
    For roads and trails
And ripped my forest
    For trams and timber.
They bored me with holes,
    Severed my mineral veins,
And dumped my rock
    To bleach upon the slope.
With mud and muck
    They filled the valley
And broke the silence
    With strange noises.
My face is old —
    Sore and beaten.
No longer I wish to be
    A rugged mountain
Among my untouched friends —
    But, then, I know from
What was given —
    Perhaps, a better world.

Roberts—1970

The granite mountain at Turret refuses to reveal its secrets

EARLY RANCHERS

Along a winding river
    Of a cold mountain valley,
Cattle, sheep, and horse
    Searched for new-born grass
Climbing through melting snow.
    Clem, in his rock-wall cabin,
High and beyond,
    Thought of a blood-red steak,
A side of mutton, and a
    Horse to carry winter ore.
Little is known and less
    Is scribed of these men of
Cattle, sheep, and horse,
    Who fed the towns and camps
Of Leadville, Cripple Creek, and
    A hundred more.

Roberts—1972

Isolated ranches supplied many mining towns of the Rockies

Cattle and horses were once his concern

Barns and sheds were built like ranch houses in the early days

Abandoned railroad bed to Eureka in the San Juans

Pennsylvania Mine in Peru Creek

Wall logs project into the San Juan landscape and cloudy sky at Alta

Alone among debris of brick and broken timber

A wheel, a tongue, both in someone's antique shop

GHOSTS

Sagging doors swing in winds,
    Rains incise yellow dumps,
Rusting ore cars, rails, and cables
    Lie in green acid waters, and
Furrowed trails are lost in
    The pine and aspen.
Bleached boards with square nails
    Are turned to stormy skies.
Rimless wheels rest against
    A falling wall.
A weathered headstone reads,
    "Born January 3, Died January 5, 1862."
Decaying timbers harbor the termite,
    And chipmunks nest in rotten logs.
Old cabins with saddle backs,
    And titled, frameless windows
Die in the green meadow.
    Only ghosts race now among
The mountains, valleys, and timber.

Roberts—1972

Ghosts at Independence townsite

As families grew so did cabins

Along the main street of Nevadaville

Winter snows were too heavy

On the mountain road ore wagons crossed Argentine Pass and the Continental Divide at 13,132 feet

Highland Mary Mine gazes upon a valley from above timberline

A failure looks across the valley to the snowcapped Sangre de Cristo Mountains

The Josephine in Stevens Gulch

Interlocking timbers retain mill tailings near Romley

High on a valley wall, a mine that survived falling rocks and snowslides

Empty kitchen where sourdough bread and biscuits were baked for hungry miners of Rosita

Only ore-car tracks now lead to the mine dump

Rotting timbers of a mine portal

A trackless trestle to the ore bin

Brick furnace at Sellar's Meadow

Vibrating ribbed table separated fine gold from crushed rock

It once gave protection to a prospector in the Mosquito Range

It could be in Greece, but instead, a once coking oven at Redstone

Sagging cables to the Mountain Top Mine in Governor Basin, San Juan Mountains

Men pushed and mules pulled these ore cars

Leftovers of a gold-placer operation

Ore cars rest in acid water and mud at the Bassick Mine

Afternoon shadows in Eureka in the San Juans

Rock waste from a deep mine

Yellowing dump that still claims gold values

Stone corners were set and surveyed to mark claim boundaries

Doors still swing on this hundred-year-old barn

Cold-storage pantry in square-nail days

In ground-blizzard country, snow fences were important

Once a corral for stagecoach horses on Boreas Pass

Steps to a once warm house at Tomboy in the San Juans

Collapsed walkway from mill to mine in the high country of Alta Lakes

In 1874, the court house in Fairplay witnessed many legal complexities

A MINER'S HOLIDAY

Soiled cigars and
     Soggy cigarettes
Floated on whiskey and gin
     In dented cans among
Bottles of beer and wine
     In Nellie's tent saloon
Down by the river.
     The happy Pole draped
The table and smiled.
     Big Swede, with toothless
Grin and broken nose,
     Lifted a battered hat —
Wished the barmaid well,
     Then slipped under the table
For a miner's holiday.

Roberts—1972

Boiler, machine, and compressor shop near timberline in Buckskin Creek

THE VEIN

Hammer echoes bounced
    Along the tunnel line, and
Sparks of yellow sprang from
    Tempered steel that holed
The banded rock.
    Crystals in wandering veins
Pierced the icy darkness,
    Water flowed from roof
And wall, and purple haze
    From powder smoke
Rested against the floor.
    Pete Stavinsky, of a distant
Land, was cold and wet —
    Then a hundred ton came
Crashing down
    To hide the Nameless Mine — and Pete.

Roberts—1972

120

Mineralized vein follows an opening in the country rock

Ore bucket that no longer rolls on wheels

Early travelers sometimes prodded oxen across plains and mountains

In the winter, covered with 12 feet of snow

Gravity did all the work

Brick-rock stack of an early smelter near Blackhawk

In 1909, it swung and creaked with the winds of Seaton Mountain

In silence and respect, the Highland Mary Mill clings tenaciously to the valley wall

Grinding crushers no longer disturb the gulch

A lonely sentinel guards Cripple Creek and Mount Pisgah

Many mining towns like Nevadaville, rest silently in their vacuum

Mill tailings spread into a wooded valley of the San Juan Mountains

Steps leading to nowhere

Stone wall and window in Russell Gulch

As ice thickened, drainage outlets were lowered in this oak-staved barrel at the Hilltop Mine

Among timber and brick, a flumed boiler survived the snowslide

SOMEONE'S ALWAYS 'ROUND

Among pine and fir,
    On crests of clouds, and
In tumbling snow
    Falling with the wind, and
On boiling streams —
    In the rocks,
On the beaver pond, and
    With the nodding lily
In the meadow —
    Someone's always 'round
To hear, to listen, to know.

Roberts—1972

In a forest of Engelmann Spruce, Father Dyer made a home in the 1870's

Sts. Johns in the summer of 1971

In 1972, the house front (right, above) had partially collapsed

Winds from Saint Mary's Glacier know this window in the town of Ninety Four

The Superintendent's office

The Prospector's office

A glacial stream from a bay window at Animas Forks

Broken tram cable against a stormy sky in the San Juans

Socrates wonders about the supports

A famous Halloween trick even in the early days

Temporary monument to more active days

Wooden dam that no longer serves a purpose

An early day something-or-other

*No longer are these oil (a) and
carbide (b) mine lamps used*

a

b

Warped shakes held by square nails for a hundred years

From such mills came high values of gold and silver of the Silvercliff area

147

There will always be those that destroy

Early fences were of locked logs

Ghosts of an 1878 mining-camp kitchen

Railroad grade above timberline to the summit of Mount McClellan near Waldorf

In 1873, the Hilltop Mine (13,500') in the Mosquito Range surfaced high values of lead, zinc, copper, and silver

151

No fancy plumbing in those days

Tumbling brick walls and twisted steel of a furnace at the Tomboy Mill

As time passes, more timbers fall into the lake

Decaying log dam of a reservoir that supplied water for downstream gold-placer operations

Restaurant that no longer serves lunch in Silver Plume

Little remains of a famous powerhouse at Crystal

Track and air line enter the portal of the abandoned Stevens Mine

At Redstone, tons of coking coal were fed into these beehive furnaces

Through a paneless window, several cabins at Ashcroft

NO CHOICE

She danced and whirled
    Across the crowded floor
And knew
    There'd be a miner's call
To share his sweat and grime
    And heavy sour-dough bread
At coffee-breakfast time.

Roberts—1971

Where once something was always happening

Time is a professional sculptress

A roof at Sts. Johns

Projecting into space toward Sheep Mountain

A mill looks upon the ghosts of Ula

Just cover us again

THE CAMP DUMP

Cast from windows and doors
    Decades ago and labels
Long gone,
    We rust among
Broken bottles, blackened leather,
    And bleached bones
Scattered down the slope by those

    Who searched our skeletons
For antique shops.
    We rested years
In peace below the soil
    And in shadows of the fir —
Again we ask for cover.

              Roberts—1972

GIVE A THOUGHT

Walls are bleached and breeched and
    Roof shakes, loose and warped,
Lie scattered.
    Square nails are buried
In rafters, floors, and tilted sills.
    Winds and rains
Have long rutted streets and
    Carried the dust beyond.
Now across the grass and
    In ravines — beer cans,
Plastic plates, and broken bottles
    Are the "flowers" of an
Old town once proud and clean
    In a mountain valley torn
By four-wheel vehicles and
    Sputtering motor bikes.

Roberts—1972

No comment

In the summer, cattle seek its shade

Where only wind whistles are heard

Walter lived in a spruce log cabin

Many went young in those days

Through a skeleton, a famous school in Russell Gulch

Standing in 1970 — collapsed in 1971

Cans, pipes, wheels, and track are all a part

Even a tree cannot survive storms at Tabasco

Floresta coal brought many miners to a rugged country

Little remains at Waldorf except the view

Glaciated mountains look on relics of the Tomboy Mine in the San Juans

A doomed cabin of spruce board at Turret

A prospector was warm in winter, cool in summer, and rattlesnakes were always a problem

Just a matter of time

So small is man and what he does

Sled that carried many logs of Englemann Spruce

Silent silhouette against a restless sky

It offered warmth above timberline to isolated miners

Trains across South Park were repaired in this round house at Como

Stop to hear
  The wilderness listen, then
See light birthed by darkness,
  And shadows fuse with
Time in reflecting waters.
            Roberts—1971

Sunset at the South London Mine

GENERAL LOCATION OF PHOTOGRAPHS

(Refer to Plat Book of Colorado, published by W. W. Hixson & Co., Rockford, Illinois. Mileages given for locations are bearing-scaled distances and *not* road distances).

1 — Above Sacramento Camp, Park Co., 8/72, LWL.

3 — Mount Lincoln, north of Alma, Park Co.; 1/73, LWL.

4 — Southeast of Marble, Purple Mountain in background, Gunnison Co., 8/72, JJF.

5 — Yankee Boy Basin, 7 miles west of Ouray, Ouray Co., 8/71, JJF.

6 — Yule Pass, 5 miles southeast of Marble, Gunnison Co., 8/72, JJF.

7 — Looking south into Hall Valley from the Continental Divide, Park Co., 8/71, JJF.

9 — Mount Democrat (14,142') at head of Buckskin Creek and 6 miles northwest of Alma, Park Co., 9/72, DAL.

10 — Head of Stevens Gulch (12,500'), 5.5 mles southwest of Silver Plume, Clear Creek Co., 9/70, LWL.

11 — Same location as 10, 9/70, LWL.

12 — Bunkhouse at San Juan Chief Mill near Mineral Point, 7 miles east of Ouray, San Juan Co., 7/71, JJF.

13 — Tomboy Mill in Savage Basin (11,520'), 4 miles east of Telluride, San Miguel Co., 9/72, DAL.

14 — On east slope of Mount Bross at 11,260' and 3 miles northwest of Alma, Park Co., 7/71, LWL.

15 — Four miles north of Bonanza; Flagstaff Mountain in background, Saguache Co., 5/72, JJF.

16 — Sketch, near summit of Weston Pass, Park Co., 5/71, DAL.

17 — Ashcroft, 8 miles south of Aspen, Pitkin Co., 5/72, JJF.

18 — Sketch, North Empire, Clear Creek Co., 4/71, DAL.

19 — (top). Fairplay, Park Co., 1/73, LWL.

19 — (bottom). Just east of Highway 285 and 14 miles south of Fairplay, Park Co., 5/71, LWL.

20 — Homestead Subdivision on Highway 285 and 10 miles southwest of Morrison, Jefferson Co., 8/72, LWL.

21 — Four miles southwest of Alma, Park Co., 9/72, LWL.

22 — (top). Near Guston, 12 miles north of Silverton, Ouray Co., 8/71, JJF.

22 — (bottom). Same location at 13, 7/71, JJF.

23 — (top). Near Gunsight Pass, 4 miles northwest of Crested Butte, Gunnison Co., 8/72, JJF.

23 — (bottom). At Coeur d'Alene Mine, Central City, Gilpin Co., 8/72, DAL.

24 — At Eureka townsite, 8.5 miles northeast of Silverton and on Animas River, San Juan Co., 9/72, LWL.

25 — Same location as 22 (top), 8/71, JJF.

26 — Nevadaville, 2.5 miles southwest of Central City, Gilpin Co., 3/71, LWL.

27 — Above timberline (11,840') and above Sacramento campsite, 6 miles west of Fairplay, Park Co., 7/72, DAL.

28 — At Sts. Johns, 2 miles southwest of Montezuma, Summit Co., 9/72, JJF.

29 — Hoist from Mountain Top Mine, Governor Basin, 7 miles west of Ouray, Ouray Co., 8/71, JJF.

30 — Sunnyside Mill at Eureka, 8 miles south of Silverton, San Juan Co., 7/71, JJF.

31 — Same location as 28, 9/72, JJF.

32 — (top). Two miles north of Silvercliff, Custer Co., 3/71, DAL.

32 — (bottom). Along Highway 285, 14 miles south of Fairplay, Park Co., 3/71, DAL.

33 — Hilltop Mine, near crest of Mosquito Range and 9 miles west of Fairplay and up Four Mile Creek, Park Co., 7/71, LWL.

34 — Sketch, Salina, Boulder Co., 8/71, DAL.

35 — Same location as 26, 3/71, LWL.

36 — Same location as 28, 9/72, JJF.

37 — North of Victor 1.5 miles, Teller Co., 7/71, LWL.

38 — Same location as 13, 9/72, LWL.

39 — Above Bridal Vail Falls, 2 miles east of Telluride, San Miguel Co., 9/72, LWL.

40 — (top). Same location as 12, 7/71, JJF.

40 — (bottom). Two miles east of Cripple Creek, Teller Co., 7/71, LWL.

41 — London Mountain, west of Alma, Park Co., 1/72, LWL.

42 — Same location as 47, 7/72, LWL.

43 — Eight miles west of Fairplay at Sacramento campsite, Park Co., 8/70, LWL.

44 — Camp Bird No. 3 Mine, Imogene Basin, 6 miles southwest of Ouray, Ouray Co., 9/72, LWL.

45 — Animas Forks, 12 miles northeast of Silverton, San Juan Co., 8/71, JJF.

46 — Sketch, above Sacramento, 6 miles west of Fairplay, Park Co., 8/72, DAL.

47 — (top). On crest of Horseshoe Peak, Mosquito Range and 10.5 miles slightly south-west of Fairplay, Park Co., 7/71, LWL.

47 — (bottom). Near Turret, Chaffee Co., 6/71, LWL.

48 — At Turret, 10 miles north of Salida, Chaffee Co., 7/71, JJF.

49 — Sneffels, 6 miles west of Ouray, Ouray Co., 7/71, JJF.

50 — House at Crystal, 4.5 miles east of Marble, Gunnison Co., 5/72, JJF.

51 — Near summit of Weston Pass, Park Co., 5/71, LWL.

53 — Argentine Mill (10,840') in Peru Creek, 4 miles northeast of Montezuma, Summit Co., 7/71, LWL.

54 — Same location as 12, 7/71, JJF.

55 — Same location as 49, 7/71, JJF.

56 — (top). Fairplay, Park Co., 1/73, LWL.

56 — (bottom). One mile north of Howardsville on Animas River, San Juan Co., 9/72, LWL.

57 — Near Gladstone on Cement Creek and 7 miles north of Silverton, San Juan Co., 9/72, LWL.

58 — Operating Pandora Mill, 2 miles east of Telluride, San Miguel Co., 9/72, LWL.

59 — Two miles north of Silverton, San Juan Co., 7/71, JJF.

60 — Red Mountain Town near Red Mountain Pass, Ouray Co., 8/71, JJF.

61 — Near Yankee Girl Mine at Guston, Ouray Co., 8/71, JJF.

62 — On east slope (12,000') of Mount Bross, 3 miles northwest of Alma, Park Co., 9/72, LWL.

63 — On south slope (11,200') of Peru Creek and below Pennsylvania Mine, 4 miles northeast of Montezuma, Summit Co., 7/71, LWL.

64 — Two miles north of Silvercliff, Custer Co., 8/71, DAL.

65 — Nevadaville, 2 miles southwest of Central City, Gilpin Co., 12/71, JJF.

66 — Portland Mine at Cripple Creek, Teller Co., 8/72, JJF.

67 — Same location as 22, 8/71, JJF.

68 — Sketch, at Ula, 4 miles north of Silvercliff, Custer Co., 5/70, DAL.

69 — (top). On Colorado School of Mines Campus, Golden, 7/71, LWL.

69 — (bottom). Three miles west of Alma and in Buckskin Creek, Park Co., 9/72, LWL.

71 — Same location as 44, 9/72, LWL.

72 — Same location as 44, 9/72, LWL.

73 — Monte Cristo Mill at Breckenridge, Summit Co., 6/72, JJF.

74 — (top). On Swan River near Tiger, northeast of Breckenridge, Summit Co., 7/71, LWL.

74 — (bottom). Three miles southeast of Fairplay, Park Co., 11/71, LWL.

75 — Above Bridal Vail Falls, 2 miles east of Telluride, 9/72, DAL.

77 — (top). Same location as 21, 9/72, LWL.

77 — (bottom). Same location as 21, 9/72, LWL.

79 — At Turret 10 miles north of Salida, Chaffee Co., 1/71, LWL.

81 — Along Tarryall Creek, 25 miles southeast of Jefferson, Park Co., 5/71, LWL.

82 — (top). In northwestern Colorado near the Wyoming Line, 8/71, LWL.

82 — (bottom). Same location as above, 8/71, LWL.

83 — On Animas River near Eureka, 8 miles northeast of Silverton, San Juan Co., 9/72, LWL.

84 — Sketch, Peru Creek, 4 miles northeast of Montezuma, Summit Co., 7/71, DAL.

85 — At Alta (11,040'), 4 miles southwest of Telluride, San Miguel Co., 9/72, LWL.

86 — Same location as 44, 9/72, LWL.

87 — Same location as 23, (bottom), 8/72, DAL.

89 — Independence townsite, 3.5 miles west of Independence Pass, Pitkin Co., 8/71, LWL.

90 — Same location as 47 (bottom), 5/71, LWL.

91 — Same location as 26, 3/71, Gilpin Co., LWL.

92 — (top). West of Apex, 1.5 miles, Gilpin Co., 8/72, DAL.

92 — (bottom). Same location as 53, 9/71, JJF.

93 — (top). Highland Mary Mine, 5 miles up Cunningham Gulch, San Juan Co., 6/72, JJF.

93 — (bottom). Northeast of Silvercliff, Custer Co., 3/71, LWL.

94 — Josephine Mine in Stevens Gulch, Clear Creek Co., 9/70, JJF.

95 — At Romley, 4 miles south of St. Elmo, Chaffee Co., 7/72, JJF.

96 — Looking westward across Buckskin Creek from road to Mineral Springs, 2 miles northwest of Alma, Park Co., 5/71, LWL.

97 — At Rosita, 7.5 miles southeast of Silvercliff, Custer Co., 5/71, DAL.

98 — North of Victor 2 miles, Teller Co., 9/70, LWL.

99 — West of Alma and 5 miles up Buckskin Creek, Park Co., 9/72, LWL.

100 — Same location as 18, Clear Creek Co., 6/71, LWL.

101 — Sellar's Meadow coke oven on road from Hagerman Pass to Ruedi, Pitkin Co., 8/71, JJF.

102 — Same location as 96, 8/72, LWL.

103 — Same location as 33, 7/71, LWL.

104 — At Redstone, Pitkin Co., 8/71, LWL.

105 — Same location as 29, 8/71, JJF.

106 — Sketch, Colorado School of Mines Museum, Golden, DAL.

107 — (top). Same location as 18, 6/71, LWL.

107 — (bottom). Bassick Mill at Querida, 6 miles east of Silvercliff, Custer Co., 3/71, LWL.

108 — Same location as 24, 8/71, JJF.

109 — North of Victor 2 miles, Teller Co., 5/70, LWL.

110 — Same location as 109, 4/70, LWL.

111 — On east slope of Mount Bross and 3 miles northwest of Alma, Park Co., 8/70, LWL.

112 — Northeast of Denver—Salt Lake Railroad crossing on road to Gross Dam, Boulder, Co., 10/72, LWL.

113 — Near Puma City site on Tarryall Creek, Park Co., 3/71, LWL.

114 — (top). Somewhere in northcentral Colorado, 8/71, LWL.

114 — (bottom). South of Boreas Pass summit, Summit Co., 7/71, LWL.

115 — Same location as 13, 8/71, JJF.

116 — At Alta Lakes (11,216'), 4 miles southwest of Telluride, San Miguel Co., 9/72, LWL.

117 — At Fairplay, Park Co., 1/73, LWL.

119 — West of Alma and 6 miles up Buckskin Creek, Park Co., 9/72, LWL.

121 — In Golden Gate Canyon, near Golden, Jefferson Co., 1/73, LWL.

122 — (top). At Pennsylvania Mine, Peru Creek and 3.5 miles northeast of Montezuma, Summit Co., 7/70, LWL.

122 — (bottom). Above ranch gate in northern part of San Luis Valley, Saguache Co., 5/70, LWL.

123 — Just east of Kite Lake, 6.5 miles up Buckskin Creek west of Alma, Park Co., 9/72, DAL.

124 — Smuggler Mine, Silverplume, Clear Creek Co., 1/73, JJF.

125 — On Highway 119 and .5 mile west of Blackhawk, Gilpin Co., 12/70, LWL.

126 — At Tropic Mine, south side of Seaton Mountain 2 miles north of Idaho Springs, Clear Creek Co., 8/70, LWL.

127 — Same location as 93 (top), 6/72, JJF.

128 — Sketch, Gamble Gulch, Gilpin Co., 8/72, DAL.

129 — East of Cripple Creek, Teller Co., 9/72, JJF.

130 — At Nevadaville, 2 miles southwest of Central City, Gilpin Co., 3/71, LWL.

131 — Camp Bird Mine, 5 miles southwest of Ouray, Ouray Co., 8/70, LWL.

132 — Same location as 122 (top), 9/71, JJF.

133 — In Russell Gulch, 2 miles south of Central City, Gilpin Co., 8/72, LWL.

134 — Hilltop Mine, 9 miles west of Fairplay, Park Co., 7/71, LWL.

135 — Same location as 122 (top), 7/71, LWL.

137 — At Dyerville, 2 miles west of Boreas Pass summit, Summit Co., 7/21, LWL.

138 — (top). Same location as 28, 8/71, JJF.

138 — (bottom). Same location as 28, 9/72, JJF.

139 — Ninety-Four townsite, 8 miles northwest of Idaho Springs, Clear Creek Co., 8/71, JJF.

140 — North of Victor 2 miles, Teller Co., 8/70, LWL.

141 — Calumet Mine area, 10 miles north of Salida and 2 miles east of Turret, Chaffee Co., 5/71, LWL.

142 — Same location as 45, 7/71, JJF.

143 — Same location as 22, 7/71, JJF.

144 — (top). Location same as 140, 8/70, LWL.

144 — (bottom). Location same as 140, 8/70, LWL.

145 — (top). Same location as 13, 7/71, JJF.

145 — (bottom). Same location as 13, 7/71, JJF.

146 — Miscellaneous sketches, DAL.

147 — (top). Same location as 43, 8/70, LWL.

147 — (bottom). Same location as 32, 3/71, LWL.

148 — Dudley, 1 mile north of Alma, Park Co., 2/73, LWL.

149 — (top). Near Alma, Park Co., 2/73, LWL.

149 — (bottom). Same location as 43, 8/72, LWL.

150 — Abandoned railroad grade north of Waldorf, Clear Creek Co., 8/71, JJF.

151 — Same location as 134, Park Co., 8/70, LWL.

152 — Same location as 79, 1/71, LWL.

153 — Same location as 13, 9/72, LWL.

154 — Same location as 116, 9/72, LWL.

155 — On Tarryall Creek, 3 miles northwest of Como, Park, Co., 7/71, LWL.

156 — Silver Plume, Clear Creek Co., 11/70, JJF.

157 — Sheep Mountain Tunnel Powerhouse, Gunnison, Co., 6/72, JJF.

158 — (top). Stevens Mine, 3 miles up Stevens Gulch from Graymont on Highway 6, Clear Creek Co., 8/70, LWL.

158 — (bottom). Same location as 104, 8/71, LWL.

159 — Same location as 17, 5/71, JJF.

161 — Same location as 19 (bottom), 5/71, LWL.

162 — Same location as 17, 6/72, JJF.

163 — Same location as 28, 9/72, JJF.

164 — (top). In the Mosquito Range, 6 miles west of Fairplay, Park Co., 9/70, LWL.

164 — (bottom). At Ula, 3 miles north of Silvercliff, Custer Co., 3/71, LWL.

165 — Same location as 43, 8/72, LWL.

167 — Carson, 9 miles southwest of Lake City, Hinsdale Co., 8/72, JJF.

168 — (top). Same location as 19 (bottom), 5/71, LWL.

168 — (bottom). Same location as 19 (bottom), 5/71, LWL.

169 — Central City Cemetery, I mile west of Central City, Gilpin Co., 9/72, LWL.

170 — Nevadaville Cemetery, 3.5 miles west of Central City, Gilpin Co., 9/72, LWL.

171 — (top). Same location as 26, 8/71, LWL.

171 — (bottom). On shelf road to Cinnamon Pass, 20 miles west of Lake City, Hinsdale Co., 7/70, JJF.

172 — (top). Same location as 22, 8/71, JJF.

172 — (bottom). Tabasco Mine bunkhouse, Hinsdale Co., 8/71, JJF.

173 — (top). Floresta, near Kebler Pass, Animas Co., 7/72, JJF.

173 — (bottom). Waldorf site, Clear Creek Co., 8/71, JJF.

174 — Same location as 13, 8/71, JJF.

175 — Same location as 79, 5/71, LWL.

176 — Same location as 141, Chaffee Co., 5/71, LWL.

177 — Same location as 22 (top), 8/71, JJF.

178 — Same location as 10, 10/71, DAL.

179 — Below Fire Lookout Station on Squaw Peak, Clear Creek Co., 7/70, LWL.

180 — (top). In Russell Gulch, 3.5 miles southwest of Central City, Gilpin Co., 8/72, LWL.

180 — (bottom). On east slope of Mount Bross and 3 miles northwest of Alma, Park Co., 10/72, LWL.

181 — At Como, Park Co., 1/73, LWL.

182 — Same location as 53, 7/71, LWL.

183 — (top). At summit of Weston Pass, Park Co., 7/70, LWL.

183 — (bottom). Same location as 53, 7/71, LWL.

184 — South London Mine, 7 miles west of Alma, Park Co., 9/72, JJF.

185 — In the Tarryall Mountains, Park Co., 6/69, LWL.